Our Favorite
Bacon
Recipes

Copyright 2022, Gooseberry Patch
Previously published under ISBN 978-1-62093-224-7
Cover: Farm-Fresh Bacon & Spinach Quiche (page 19)

Mmm...is anything better than bacon? To separate
bacon slices easily, first let the package stand at
room temperature for about 20 minutes.

Cherry Bacon Roll-Ups

Makes 6 dozen

1/2 c. butter	2 eggs, beaten
1 c. water	1/4 lb. ground beef
1/2 c. dried cherries	1/4 lb. hot ground pork sausage
2 c. herb-flavored stuffing mix	1 lb. bacon, cut into thirds

In a saucepan, melt butter in water; remove from heat. Combine cherries with stuffing. Mix butter mixture with cherry mixture in a large bowl. Blend well; chill one hour. Add remaining ingredients except bacon, mixing well. Shape into pecan-shaped balls; wrap with bacon, secure with toothpicks and place in a 13"x9" baking dish. Bake at 375 degrees for 35 minutes, or until bacon is crisp and beef mixture is no longer pink inside.

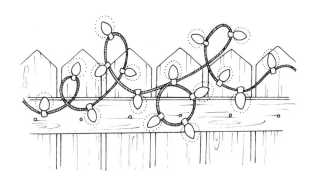

Partying outdoors? Wind sparkling white lights along
the garden fence and in the trees for a twinkling
firefly effect as the sun sets.

Bacon-Wrapped Scallops

Serves 8 to 10

1/2 c. all-purpose flour
1/2 t. salt
1-1/2 t. paprika
1/2 t. white pepper
1/2 t. garlic powder
1 egg

1 c. milk
21 scallops
1 to 2 c. dry bread crumbs
7 slices bacon, cut into thirds
Optional: remoulade sauce

Combine flour, salt, paprika, white pepper and garlic powder in a shallow dish. Beat egg and milk together in a small bowl. Roll scallops in seasoned flour, shaking off excess. Dip scallops in egg mixture, then coat with bread crumbs. Preheat oven to 400 degrees. Wrap each scallop with bacon and secure with a toothpick. Place scallops on a lightly greased baking sheet. Bake until bacon is crisp and scallops are cooked, about 20 to 25 minutes. Serve hot with remoulade sauce, if desired.

Looking for a new way to serve a favorite snack?
Retro-style plates, cake stands and chip & dip sets
really add color and fun.

Feisty Red Pepper-Bacon Dip

Makes about 2 cups

1/2 c. cream cheese, softened
8-oz. container sour cream
1 T. creamy horseradish
7-oz. jar roasted red peppers,
    drained

4 to 5 slices bacon, crisply cooked
    and crumbled
Optional: additional crumbled
    bacon, minced fresh chives
snack crackers

Combine all ingredients except crackers in a large bowl. Beat with an
electric mixer on low speed until mixed well. Cover and refrigerate for
at least one hour. Garnish with additional crumbled bacon and chives,
if desired. Serve with crackers.

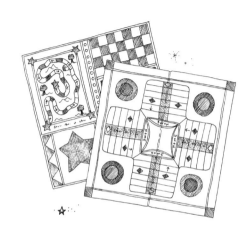

Add some vintage flair to your buffet by placing gently used
game boards under your serving dishes. Check the closet for
forgotten games or pick some up at yard sales. Cover with
self-adhesive clear plastic for wipe-clean ease.

Undefeated Bacon-Cheese Dip

Makes about 7 cups

1 lb. bacon, crisply cooked
   and crumbled
2 8-oz. pkgs. shredded Cheddar
   cheese
1/2 c. chopped pecans

2 c. mayonnaise-type salad
   dressing
1 onion, chopped
assorted crackers

Mix all ingredients together except crackers. Serve with crackers.

No peeking! Lifting the lid on the slow cooker allows heat
and moisture to escape and can delay cooking time by
15 to 20 minutes. Just remove the lid when stirring and
adding ingredients as specified by the recipe.

Club Sandwich Dip

Serves 20

1 lb. deli turkey, chopped
1/2 lb. deli ham, chopped
1/2 lb. sliced Swiss or American
  cheese, chopped
8-oz. pkg. cream cheese, cubed
1 c. mayonnaise
2 t. Dijon mustard

6 slices bacon, crisply cooked,
  crumbled and divided
1/2 c. cherry or grape tomatoes,
  chopped
toast points and assorted
  cut veggies

In a 4-quart slow cooker, combine turkey, ham, cheeses, mayonnaise and mustard. Cover and cook on high setting for one to 2 hours, until cheeses are melted, stirring after one hour. Before serving, stir in half of the bacon; garnish with remaining bacon and tomatoes. Serve warm with toast points and veggies.

Thread bite-size veggies like cherry tomatoes, whole mushrooms, yellow pepper squares and baby carrots onto skewers for tasty dipping. Stand skewers in a plump vase... it doubles as a table decoration!

Bacon-Horseradish Dip

Makes 7 to 8 cups

3 8-oz. pkgs. cream cheese, cubed and softened
12-oz. pkg. shredded Cheddar cheese
1 c. half-and-half
1/3 c. green onion, chopped
3 cloves garlic, minced
3 T. prepared horseradish
1 T. Worcestershire sauce
1/2 t. pepper
12 slices bacon, crisply cooked and crumbled
bagel chips or assorted crackers

Combine all ingredients except bacon and chips or crackers in a slow cooker. Cover and cook on low setting for 4 to 5 hours, or on high setting for 2 to 2-1/2 hours, stirring once halfway through. Stir in bacon; serve with bagel chips or crackers.

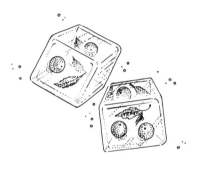

Guests are sure to appreciate pitchers of ice water they can help themselves to. Make some fancy party ice cubes by tucking sprigs of mint into ice cube trays before freezing.

Tomato-Bacon Nibbles

Makes 2 to 2-1/2 dozen

24 to 30 cherry tomatoes
1 lb. bacon, crisply cooked
   and crumbled
2 T. fresh parsley, chopped

1/2 c. green onions, finely
   chopped
3 T. grated Parmesan cheese
1/2 c. mayonnaise

Cut a thin slice off the top of each tomato. If desired, cut a thin slice from bottom of each tomato so they'll stand upright. Scoop out and discard tomato pulp; place tomatoes upside-down on a paper towel to drain for 10 minutes. Mix bacon and remaining ingredients in a small bowl; stuff tomatoes. Serve immediately, or chill up to 2 hours.

Keep party time super-simple. Serve one or two tried & true appetizers like Bacon-Wrapped Dates and your favorite cheese ball. Pick up some tasty go-withs like pickles, marinated olives and cocktails nuts at the grocery store. Relax and enjoy your guests!

Bacon-Wrapped Dates

Makes 2 to 2-1/2 dozen

1 lb. bacon
8 to 12-oz. pkg. pitted whole
   dates

Optional: 25 to 30 wooden
   toothpicks

Cut bacon slices into thirds. Wrap a piece of bacon around each date. Secure with a toothpick, if using, or wrap tightly and place seam-side down on an ungreased baking sheet. Bake at 350 degrees for 20 to 25 minutes, until bacon is crisp. Cool 10 to 15 minutes before serving.

Planning a midday brunch? Alongside breakfast foods like baked eggs, coffee cake and cereal, offer a light, savory casserole or a fresh salad for those who have already enjoyed breakfast.

Farm-Fresh Bacon & Spinach Quiche

Makes 8 servings

8 slices bacon, crisply cooked,
    crumbled and divided
9-inch frozen pie crust, thawed
2 c. shredded Monterey Jack
    cheese

10-oz. pkg. frozen chopped
    spinach, thawed and drained
1-1/2 c. milk
3 eggs, beaten
1 T. all-purpose flour

Sprinkle half of crumbled bacon on bottom of pie crust. Mix together cheese, spinach, milk, eggs and flour. Pour over crust. Sprinkle remaining crumbled bacon on top. Bake at 350 degrees for one hour, or until center is set.

Set the breakfast table the night before...
you may even get the kids to help you.
Then enjoy a relaxed breakfast in the morning.

Sunny-Side-Up Egg Pizza

Makes 6 servings

12-inch Italian pizza crust
6 eggs
1-1/2 c. shredded mozzarella
  cheese
8 slices bacon, crisply cooked
  and crumbled

1/2 c. red pepper, chopped
1/2 c. green pepper, chopped
1/2 c. onion, chopped

Place crust on a lightly greased 12" round pizza pan. With a 2-1/2" round
biscuit cutter, cut out 6 circles from crust, evenly spaced and about one inch
from the edge. Reserve cut-out crust circles for another use. Break an egg
into each hole in the crust. Sprinkle remaining ingredients over the crust.
Bake at 450 degrees for 8 to 10 minutes, until eggs are completely set.
Cut into wedges.

For the best scrambled eggs, don't skip on the whisking. Whisk until the yolks are completely blended with the whites, about 30 to 40 seconds. You'll be rewarded with soft, fluffy scrambled eggs.

Amish Breakfast Casserole

Makes 8 to 10 servings

1 lb. bacon, diced
1 sweet onion, chopped
1 green pepper, diced
10 eggs, beaten
1-1/2 c. cream-style cottage
   cheese

4 c. frozen shredded hashbrowns,
   thawed
2 c. shredded Cheddar cheese
1-1/2 c. shredded Monterey Jack
   cheese, divided

In a large skillet over medium heat, cook bacon, onion and green pepper until bacon is crisp; drain and set aside. In a large bowl, combine remaining ingredients, reserving 1/4 cup of the Monterey Jack cheese. Stir bacon mixture into egg mixture. Transfer to a greased 13"x9" baking pan; sprinkle with reserved cheese. Bake, uncovered, at 350 degrees for 35 to 40 minutes, until set and bubbly. Let stand 10 minutes before cutting.

Visit a nearby farmers' market for fresh fruits &
vegetables, baked goods, jams & jellies...perfect for
a farm-fresh breakfast!

Bacon Skillet Breakfast

Serves 2 to 4

8 slices bacon
4 potatoes, peeled and diced
1/2 c. onion, diced

4 eggs, beaten
1 c. shredded Cheddar cheese

In a skillet over medium heat, cook bacon until crisp. Remove bacon from skillet to a paper towel; add potatoes and onion to drippings in skillet. Cook potatoes and onion until tender; drain well but do not remove from skillet. In a separate non-stick skillet over low heat, scramble eggs until set but still moist. Spoon eggs over potatoes; layer with bacon and cheese. Cover and cook over low heat until cheese is melted.

Go out to greet the sunrise! Wrap warm breakfast breads
in a vintage tea towel before tucking into a basket...
add a thermos of hot coffee or tea.

Camp-Time Eggs & Bacon

Serves 10 to 12

1 lb. bacon
1 doz. eggs, beaten
1/2 c. milk

1 T. butter
1/2 to 1 c. shredded Cheddar
   cheese

In a non-stick skillet over medium heat, cook bacon until crisp. Drain bacon on a paper towel-covered plate; drain skillet. Cut bacon into 1/2-inch pieces and set aside. In a bowl, beat eggs with milk until well blended. Add butter to skillet; stir until melted. Add egg mixture; cook over medium heat until eggs are set, stirring occasionally to scramble. Turn off heat. Add bacon and desired amount of cheese; stir until cheese melts.

A Bundt® coffee cake with a flower-filled vase tucked in
the center makes a delightful centerpiece for
a casual brunch gathering.

Sugarplum Bacon

Makes 18 to 24 pieces

1/2 lb. bacon, room temperature   1 t. cinnamon
1/2 c. brown sugar, packed

Cut each slice of bacon in half crosswise. Combine brown sugar and cinnamon in a shallow bowl. Dredge each piece of bacon in brown sugar mixture; twist and place in an ungreased 13"x9" baking pan. Bake, uncovered, at 350 degrees for 15 to 20 minutes, until bacon is crisp and sugar is bubbly. Remove slices to aluminum foil to cool. Serve at room temperature.

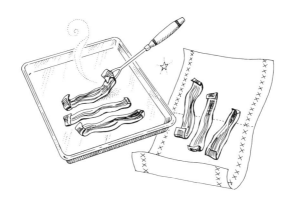

To prepare lots of crispy bacon easily, try baking it
in the oven. Place bacon slices on a broiler pan, place the pan
in a cool oven and turn the temperature to 400 degrees.
Bake for 12 to 15 minutes. Turn bacon over and bake
for another 8 to 10 minutes.

Bacon-Wrapped Egg Cups

6 thick-cut slices peppered bacon
6 eggs, beaten
1 c. sliced mushrooms
3 roma tomatoes, diced

1 green pepper, diced
1 t. garlic, minced
salt and pepper to taste

Cook bacon in a skillet over medium heat until almost crisp; drain on paper towels. Scramble eggs to desired doneness in drippings in skillet; set aside. In a bowl, combine vegetables and garlic; season with salt and pepper. Lightly grease 6 small ramekins or custard dishes. Arrange one slice of bacon around the inside of each ramekin. Evenly spoon egg mixture and vegetables into ramekins. Place a trivet in a slow cooker; put ramekins on trivet. Add water to slow cooker to a depth of about one inch. Cover and cook on high setting for 1-1/2 to 2 hours, until warmed through and vegetables are tender.

Love cheesy recipes, but want to cut down on the calories and fat? Choose reduced-fat (not fat-free) cheese, which melts well in hot dishes.

Grab & Go Breakfast Roll-Ups

Makes 6 servings

12 slices bacon
6 eggs, beaten
1/2 c. milk
1 t. garlic powder

1 T. butter
6 8-inch flour tortillas, warmed
6 slices American cheese

In a skillet over medium heat, cook bacon until crisp; drain on paper towels. Meanwhile, whisk eggs with milk and garlic powder. Heat butter in a skillet over medium-low heat; scramble eggs to desired doneness. To assemble, top each warmed tortilla with eggs, 2 slices bacon and one slice cheese. Roll up partway; fold in ends and finish rolling. Wrap each roll-up in a paper towel; tuck into a small plastic zipping bag and refrigerate. To serve, microwave for 30 to 40 seconds.

Garden-fresh berries and peaches are luscious on waffles and pancakes. Frozen fruit is good too and available all year 'round. Simmer fruit with a little sugar until it's syrupy. What a tasty way to start the day!

Bacon Griddle Cakes

Serves 4 to 6

12 slices bacon
2 c. pancake mix

Garnish: butter, maple syrup

On a griddle over medium heat, cook bacon until crisp. Drain, reserving 2 tablespoons drippings. Meanwhile, prepare pancake mix according to package directions, omitting a little of the water or milk for a thicker batter. Arrange bacon slices 2 inches apart on griddle greased with reserved drippings. Slowly pour pancake batter over each piece of bacon, covering each slice. Cook until golden on both sides; serve with butter and maple syrup.

Put a new spin on burgers! Swap out the same ol' buns with different types of bread like English muffins, Italian ciabatta or sliced French bread. Pita rounds make sandwiches that are easier for littler hands to hold.

Bacon & Blue Cheese Stuffed Burgers

Makes 4 burgers

1-1/2 lbs. ground beef
1 T. Worcestershire sauce
2 T. Dijon mustard
1/2 t. pepper
4 to 6 slices bacon, crisply cooked
    and crumbled

4-oz. container crumbled
    blue cheese
4 hamburger buns, split and
    toasted
Garnish: sliced red onion,
    sliced tomato, lettuce leaves

Combine ground beef, Worcestershire sauce, mustard and pepper. Mix lightly and form into eight, 1/4-inch thick patties. Stir together bacon and blue cheese; set aside 1/3 of mixture for topping. Spoon remaining mixture onto centers of 4 patties. Top with remaining 4 patties; press edges together to seal. Grill over medium-high heat to desired doneness, 4 to 6 minutes per side, topping with reserved bacon mixture when nearly done. Serve burgers on toasted rolls, garnished as desired.

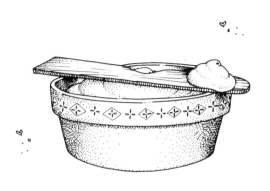

If you're making a sandwich several hours before serving, first spread a light layer of softened butter, margarine or cream cheese on the bread. This prevents the bread from absorbing the moisture from the filling and becoming soggy.

Cajun Chicken-Bacon Sandwiches

Serves 4

1/4 c. butter, melted
2 T. Cajun seasoning
4 boneless, skinless chicken
 breasts
4 slices Pepper Jack cheese

4 sandwich buns, split
8 slices bacon, crisply cooked
Optional: lettuce, mayonnaise,
 sliced tomato

Melt butter in a large skillet over medium heat; stir in Cajun seasoning. Add chicken; cook until juices run clear when pierced with a fork. Top chicken with cheese; allow to melt. Serve on buns topped with bacon and, if desired, lettuce, mayonnaise and tomato slices.

Bite-size mini sandwiches make an easy, tasty addition to
any casual dinner or party buffet. Whip up some grilled cheese,
BLT, Reuben or other favorite sandwiches, then cut them
into small squares. Top with an olive or a pickle slice
and spear with party picks.

Chicken-Apple Sliders

Makes 8 servings

1 Granny Smith apple, cored
   and shredded
1/4 c. celery, finely chopped
1/2 t. poultry seasoning
1/4 t. salt
1/4 t. pepper
2 T. honey
1 lb. ground chicken

8 slices bacon, crisply cooked,
   crumbled and divided
Optional: 2 slices favorite cheese,
   quartered
8 slider rolls, split and toasted
Garnish: mayonnaise, shredded
   lettuce, sliced tomato
   and onion

In a large bowl, combine apple, celery and seasonings; toss to mix. Add honey, chicken and half of bacon. Stir until combined; do not overmix. Form into 8 small patties. Grill or pan-fry patties about 4 minutes on each side, until chicken is no longer pink. If desired, top with a piece of cheese during the last few minutes of cooking. Place patties on rolls; top with remaining bacon and other toppings, as desired.

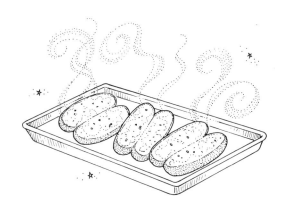

Toast sandwich buns before adding juicy fillings...it only
takes a minute and make such a tasty difference.
Buns will drip less too!

Bacon Cheeseburger Sloppy Joes

6 slices bacon
1 lb. ground turkey
1/3 c. mayonnaise
1/4 c. catsup
1 T. pickle relish

1 T. mustard
2 t. Worcestershire sauce
6 hamburger buns, split
6 slices Monterey Jack cheese
6 T. French fried onions

In a skillet over medium heat, cook bacon until crisp; set bacon aside on a paper towel. Partially drain drippings in skillet. Add turkey; cook until browned. Stir in mayonnaise, catsup, relish, mustard and Worcestershire sauce; heat through. To serve, top each bun with one cheese slice, one tablespoon onions, one slice bacon and some of the turkey mixture.

Back-Wrapped Burgers are so deliciously juicy! To keep that juice from dripping, wrap individual servings in aluminum foil, then peel back as they're eaten.

Bacon-Wrapped Burgers

Makes 6 servings

1-1/2 lbs. ground beef	1/2 t. dried rosemary
1/2 t. salt	3 T. catsup
1/4 t. pepper	3 T. water
2 T. fresh basil, chopped	6 slices bacon

Combine all ingredients except bacon in a bowl. Form the mixture into 6 patties, 3-1/2 inches in diameter and one-inch thick. Wrap a bacon slice around each and secure with a small metal skewer or toothpick. Broil or grill patties 5 inches from heat for 5 minutes on each side for medium doneness. Remove skewers or toothpicks before serving.

Which apple is best? The tastiest apples for salads and sandwiches are McIntosh, Red Delicious, Empire and Gala.

Peanut Butter Apple-Bacon Sandwiches

Makes 4 sandwiches

8 slices applewood smoked bacon
8 slices whole-grain bread
1/4 c. peach preserves
1 to 2 apples, cored and thinly
  sliced

1/4 c. creamy peanut butter
2 to 3 T. butter, softened and
  divided

In a skillet over medium heat, cook bacon until crisp; drain bacon on paper towels. Spread 4 slices of bread with preserves; layer apple and bacon slices over preserves. Spread remaining bread slices with peanut butter; close sandwiches. Spread tops of sandwiches with half of butter. Place sandwiches butter-side down on a griddle over medium heat. Spread remaining butter on unbuttered side of sandwiches. Cook 2 to 3 minutes per side, until bread is toasted and sandwiches are heated through. Serve warm.

Pick up a stack of vintage-style plastic burger baskets.
Lined with paper napkins, they're fun for serving all kinds of
sandwich meals. Clean-up is a snap too...just toss the napkins!

Chicken-Bacon Quesadillas

Serves 2 to 4

3 to 4 slices bacon
1/2 c. cooked chicken, diced
1 T. onion, chopped
1 T. green pepper, diced

2 10-inch flour tortillas
3/4 c. shredded Mexican-blend
   cheese, divided

In a large skillet, cook bacon until crisp; crumble and drain on paper towels. To drippings in skillet, add chicken, onion and pepper; cook until vegetables are crisp-tender and chicken is warmed through. Place one tortilla in a separate ungreased skillet over medium heat; top with half the cheese. Place chicken mixture and bacon on top of cheese; top with remaining cheese and remaining tortilla. Cook until cheese begins to melt and bottom tortilla is crisp. Flip and cook other side until crisp, about 5 minutes. Remove from pan and cut into wedges to serve.

Can't remember if you've already tried a recipe?
Next time, draw a little smiley face in the page's margin...
you'll remember that it was a hit!

Potato-Bacon Chowder

Makes 6 servings

2 c. potatoes, peeled and cubed
1 c. onion, chopped
1 c. water
8 slices bacon
10-3/4 oz. can cream of
   chicken soup

1 c. sour cream
2 c. milk
1/2 t. salt
1/8 t. pepper

In a large saucepan over medium heat, cook potatoes and onion in water until tender, 10 to 15 minutes. Do not drain. Meanwhile, in a large skillet over medium heat, cook bacon until crisp; drain and set aside. In a bowl, whisk together soup, sour cream and milk. Add soup mixture to potato mixture along with crumbled bacon, salt and pepper. Heat through over low heat; do not boil.

A wide-mouthed thermos is terrific for keeping soup fresh and delicious. To keep the thermos hot until lunchtime, fill it with hot water, then empty it just before adding the piping-hot soup.

Cheesy Bacon-Wild Rice Soup

9 to 10 slices bacon, diced
1 onion, chopped
2 10-3/4 oz. cans cream of
  potato soup

1-1/2 c. prepared wild rice
2 pts. half-and-half
2 c. American cheese, shredded

In a skillet over medium heat, sauté bacon and onion together until bacon is crisp and onion is tender; drain and set aside. Combine soup and rice in a saucepan; stir in bacon mixture, half-and-half and cheese. Cook over low heat until cheese melts.

A toasty touch for soups! Butter bread slices and cut into shapes using mini cookie cutters. Place on a baking sheet and bake at 425 degrees until crisp.

Bacon-Cheeseburger Soup

Serves 8 to 10

3 T. olive oil
2 onions, chopped
3 T. garlic, minced
4-oz. can sliced mushrooms,
    drained
1-1/2 lbs. ground beef
2 T. seasoning salt
8 redskin potatoes, cubed

4-1/2 c. water
2 cubes beef bouillon
5 c. milk or half-and-half, divided
2 T. all-purpose flour
3 T. bacon bits
32-oz. pkg. pasteurized process
    cheese spread, cubed
Garnish: shredded Swiss cheese

Heat oil in a large skillet over medium heat. Add onions, garlic and mushrooms; cook until onions are translucent. Add ground beef; sprinkle with seasoning salt. Cook until beef is browned; drain and set aside. Combine potatoes, water and beef bouillon in a large soup pot over medium heat. Simmer, stirring occasionally, until potatoes are tender, 10 to 15 minutes. Add 4 cups milk or half-and-half; bring to a simmer over medium heat. Add beef mixture; return to a simmer. In a small bowl, mix together flour and remaining milk until smooth. Gradually add to soup. Stir in bacon bits and cheese spread, stirring until melted and smooth. Ladle into bowls; garnish with Swiss cheese.

Top bowls of hot soup with plain or cheesy popcorn
instead of croutons for a crunchy surprise.

Creamy Split Pea Soup

Serves 8

1 lb. bacon, diced, crisply cooked
    and 2 to 3 T. drippings reserved
1 onion, diced
2 stalks celery, diced
8 c. water
16-oz. pkg. dried split peas

2 potatoes, peeled and diced
2 t. salt
1/4 t. pepper
3 cubes beef bouillon
1 bay leaf
1 c. half-and-half

Heat reserved bacon drippings in a large soup pot; sauté onion and celery over medium heat until tender. Add remaining ingredients except half-and-half; bring to a boil over medium-high heat. Reduce heat to low; cover and simmer for 45 minutes, until peas are very tender. Discard bay leaf. Fill a blender 3/4 full with soup; blend to purée. Return to soup pot; stir in half-and-half. Simmer over medium heat for 5 minutes, until heated through. Serve with reserved bacon on top.

Enjoy a favorite long-simmering recipe more often...let a slow cooker do the work! Brown and drain ground meat first, then toss all ingredients into the slow cooker. A soup that cooks for 2 hours on the stovetop can cook all day on the low setting without burning or overcooking.

Farmstand Bacon-Corn Soup

Serves 8

1 butternut squash
12 slices bacon, diced
1 onion, chopped
1 stalk celery, chopped
1 T. all-purpose flour
14-1/2 oz. can chicken broth
2 14-3/4 oz. cans creamed corn

2 8-oz. cans corn, drained
1 pt. half-and-half
1 T. fresh parsley, minced
1-1/2 t. salt
1/2 t. pepper
Optional: sour cream

Place squash on an ungreased baking sheet. Bake at 375 degrees for one hour. Cut in half; cool. Remove seeds with a spoon; scoop out pulp and mash. Set aside. In a large saucepan over medium-high heat, cook bacon until crisp. Remove bacon to paper towels, reserving 2 tablespoons drippings in saucepan. Sauté onion and celery until tender. Stir in flour; blend well. Gradually stir in 6 cups squash and remaining ingredients except sour cream; return crumbled bacon to saucepan. Cook and stir over low heat until heated through. Garnish with dollops of sour cream, if desired.

If canned beans don't agree with you, just drain and
rinse them before using...you'll be washing away
any "tinny" taste too.

Quick Bean & Bacon Soup

Makes 6 servings

1/2 lb. bacon, diced
1 onion, diced
1 stalk celery, diced
2 cloves garlic, minced

14-1/2 oz. can diced tomatoes, drained
2 15-oz. cans pork & beans
2 14-1/2 oz. cans beef broth

In a soup pot over medium heat, cook bacon until crisp. Drain most of the drippings; set aside bacon on a paper towel-lined plate. In remaining drippings, sauté onion, celery and garlic until tender. Stir in tomatoes, beans and broth; bring to a boil. Reduce heat to low; simmer, uncovered, for 15 minutes. Stir in bacon just before serving.

Have a big pot of leftover soup? Be sure to transfer the extra soup into smaller containers before refrigerating or freezing. The soup will reach a safe temperature much more quickly.

Country Beef Stew

Makes 6 to 8 servings

1/2 lb. bacon, chopped
2 lbs. stew beef cubes
1 c. onion, diced
3 to 4 stalks celery, chopped
14-1/2 oz. can diced tomatoes
3 cloves garlic, minced
1/2 t. dried sage

1/2 t. dried thyme
1/2 t. dried marjoram
2 c. beef broth
salt and pepper to taste
4 to 5 potatoes, peeled and
    quartered
4 to 5 carrots, sliced

Fry bacon in a large Dutch oven until crisp. Add beef; brown over high heat. Reduce heat to medium-low and stir in onion, celery, tomatoes with juice, garlic, sage, thyme and marjoram. Blend in beef broth, salt and pepper. Cover and simmer for 2 hours. Add potatoes and carrots. Cook an additional 30 to 40 minutes.

Cloth napkins make mealtime just a little more special...
and they're a must when serving soup. Stitch or hot-glue
fun charms to napkin rings so family members can
identify their own napkin easily.

Manhattan Clam Chowder

Serves 4 to 6

1/2 lb. bacon, chopped
1 onion, sliced
2 cloves garlic, minced
28-oz. can whole tomatoes
2 6-1/2 oz. cans minced clams
8-oz. bottle clam juice

1 T. dried thyme
salt and pepper to taste
10-oz. pkg. frozen soup
  vegetables
1 to 2 potatoes, peeled and diced

Add bacon, onion and garlic to a skillet over medium heat; cook and stir until bacon is crisp and onion is tender. Drain; add to a slow cooker. Add remaining ingredients except frozen vegetables and potatoes. Cover and cook on high setting for 2 hours. Add vegetables and potatoes. Cover; reduce heat to low and cook for 3 to 4 hours longer, until vegetables are tender.

Serving dinner for 2? No need to make rolls for 8.
Bags of frozen rolls at the grocery store let you
bake only as many as needed.

Warm Spinach & Bacon Salad

Serves 2

3 c. spinach, torn into bite-size
    pieces
1/4 c. creamy chevre cheese,
    crumbled
2 slices bacon, cut into
    1/2-inch pieces

2 t. olive oil
1 t. balsamic vinegar
salt and pepper to taste

Arrange spinach in a salad bowl; sprinkle with cheese and set aside.
Place bacon on a microwave-safe plate; microwave on high until crisp,
about 2 minutes. Reserve one teaspoon drippings in a small microwave-
safe bowl; drain bacon on paper towel and set aside. Whisk oil, vinegar,
salt and pepper into reserved drippings. Microwave, uncovered, on high
for 30 seconds, until hot. Drizzle over salad; toss to coat. Sprinkle with
reserved bacon.

A vintage-style salad that's ready to serve in seconds!
Top crisp wedges of iceberg lettuce with Thousand Island
salad dressing, diced tomato and bacon crumbles.

Asparagus, Egg & Bacon Salad

Makes 4 servings

1-2/3 c. fresh asparagus,
   trimmed and chopped
1 egg, hard-boiled, peeled
   and sliced

2 slices bacon, crisply cooked
   and crumbled

Bring a large saucepan of water to a boil over high heat. Add asparagus
and cook for 2 to 3 minutes, until crisp-tender. Drain in a colander; rinse
with cold water and let cool. Arrange asparagus on a serving plate. Top
with egg and bacon; drizzle with Vinaigrette. Serve immediately, or cover
and chill.

Vinaigrette:

1 t. extra-virgin olive oil
1 t. red wine vinegar

1/2 t. Dijon mustard
salt and pepper to taste

In a small bowl, whisk together all ingredients.

Fresh herbs will taste their best stored for just a few days in an open or perforated plastic bag in the refrigerator. To keep them up to a week, snip off the ends and arrange them in a tall glass with an inch of water. Cover loosely with a plastic bag and place in the fridge.

Avocado Coleslaw

Makes 4 to 6 servings

1 to 2 c. mayonnaise, to taste
1/2 c. mayonnaise-style salad
   dressing
2 T. sugar
1 T. white vinegar
1 t. celery seed
salt and pepper to taste
12-oz. pkg. shredded
   coleslaw mix

1/3 c. grape tomatoes, each cut
   into 3 to 4 pieces
1 avocado, halved, pitted
   and cubed
Garnish: crisply cooked and
   crumbled bacon

In a large bowl, combine mayonnaise, salad dressing, sugar, vinegar and seasonings; mix well. Add coleslaw mix and stir well. Fold in tomatoes, avocado and bacon.

Make some tangy pickled veggies next time you finish a jar of dill pickles. Simply cut up fresh carrots, green or red peppers and other vegetables, drop them into the leftover pickle juice and refrigerated for a few days.

BLT Macaroni Salad

16-oz. pkg. elbow macaroni,
    cooked
1-1/4 c. celery, diced
5 green onions, finely chopped
1 tomato, diced
1-1/4 c. mayonnaise

5 t. white vinegar
1/4 t. salt
1/8 t. pepper
1 lb. bacon, crisply cooked and
    crumbled

In a large bowl, combine macaroni, celery, onions and tomato. In a separate bowl, combine remaining ingredients except bacon; pour over macaroni mixture, tossing to coat. Cover and chill for at least 2 hours. Just before serving, sprinkle with bacon.

Tuck an apple into a bag of potatoes to keep
the potatoes from sprouting.

Country-Style Baked Potato Salad

Makes 10 to 12 servings

4 lbs. baking potatoes, peeled, cubed and cooked
1 lb. bacon, sliced into 1/2-inch pieces and crisply cooked
8-oz. pkg. shredded Cheddar cheese
1/2 c. butter, softened
1/2 c. green onions, chopped
1-1/2 c. sour cream
1 t. salt
1 t. pepper

Combine all ingredients in a large bowl, tossing gently. Chill for 2 hours before serving.

Garden-fresh vegetables are delicious prepared simply...
steamed and topped with pats of chive butter. To make, blend
1/4 cup softened butter with 2 tablespoons chopped fresh
chives, one teaspoon lemon zest and a little salt & pepper.

Great-Grandma's Green Beans

Serves 6 to 8

6 slices bacon, chopped
1 c. onion, chopped
3 T. vinegar
2 T. all-purpose flour

16-oz. pkg. frozen French-cut
   green beans
salt to taste

In a skillet over medium heat, cook bacon until crisp; remove from skillet and set aside. Add onion to drippings; cook until golden. Add vinegar and flour; stir well. Add bacon and frozen green beans; completely cover skillet with lid. Reduce heat to low. Simmer for one hour, adding a little more water or vinegar as needed. Season with salt to taste.

Enjoy seasonal fruits & veggies...strawberries and asparagus
in spring, corn and tomatoes in summer, pears and acorn
squash in fall and cabbage and apples in winter. you'll be serving
your family the tastiest, healthiest produce year 'round.

Brown Sugar-Bacon Squash

Serves 8

1 acorn squash, peeled, halved
   and seeds removed
1/3 c. butter

salt and pepper to taste
1 c. brown sugar, packed
8 slices bacon, halved

Cut each squash half into quarters and cut each quarter in half, to create 16 pieces. Place squash skin-side down on an aluminum foil-lined rimmed baking sheet. Top each piece with one teaspoon butter, salt, pepper, one tablespoon brown sugar and 1/2 slice bacon. Bake, uncovered, at 350 degrees for 30 to 45 minutes, until bacon is crisp and squash is tender.

A fun and simple meal...try a chili dog bar! Along with steamed
hot dogs and buns, set out some hot chili, shredded cheese,
sauerkraut, chopped onions and your favorite condiments.

Kansas City BBQ Beans

Serves 8 to 10

4 15-oz. cans baked beans
1/2 lb. bacon, crisply cooked
    and crumbled
1 onion, diced
1 c. dark brown sugar, packed

18-oz. bottle Kansas City-style or
    mesquite barbecue sauce
1 t. smoke-flavored cooking sauce
1/2 t. pepper

Place all ingredients in a lightly greased 13"x9" baking pan; stir until combined. Cover tightly with aluminum foil. Preheat a grill to medium-low. Place pan on grill for 20 minutes, stirring every 5 minutes to prevent scorching. Remove foil and grill another 5 to 10 minutes, until thickened. May also be baked in the oven at 400 degrees for 30 minutes; no need to stir. Uncover and bake another 5 to 10 minutes, until thickened.

After baking a casserole, save the aluminum foil covering it. Crumble the foil into a ball and use it to scrub off any baked-on cheese or sauce in the dish.

White Cheddar-Cauliflower Casserole   *Serves 6*

1 head cauliflower, cooked and
  mashed
8-oz. pkg. white Cheddar cheese,
  grated and divided
1/2 lb. bacon, crisply cooked and
  crumbled, divided

1/2 c. cream cheese, softened
2 T. sour cream
salt and pepper to taste

Combine cauliflower, half the Cheddar cheese and three-quarters of bacon
in a medium bowl. Add cream cheese and sour cream; mix well. Spread
mixture in a greased 8"x8" baking pan; top with remaining cheese and
bacon. Sprinkle with salt and pepper. Bake, uncovered, at 350 degrees
for 20 to 25 minutes, until golden around edges.

Now and then it's good to pause in our
pursuit of happiness and just be happy.

– Guillaume Apollinaire

Nana's Loaded Mashed Potatoes

Serves 8 to 10

12 potatoes, peeled and
   quartered
1/2 lb. bacon, chopped
1/2 c. butter, cubed
1/4 c. sour cream
8-oz. pkg. cream cheese, softened

8-oz. pkg. shredded sharp
   Cheddar cheese
1/2 c. green onions, chopped
salt and pepper to taste
Garnish: additional chopped
   green onions

In a stockpot over medium-high heat, cover potatoes with water. Bring to a boil over high heat and cook until fork-tender, 15 to 20 minutes. Drain well. While potatoes are cooking, cook bacon in a skillet over medium heat until crisp. Drain bacon on paper towels. Mash potatoes with butter and sour cream until creamy. Stir in bacon, cheeses, green onions, salt and pepper. Top with a sprinkle of green onions.

A clear plastic over-the-door shoe organizer is super
for pantry storage... just slip gravy mix packets,
spice jars and other small items into the pockets.

Bacon-Spinach Casserole

Serves 4

4 slices bacon, cut into bite-size
    pieces
1 onion, chopped
4-oz. pkg. sliced mushrooms
1 c. light whipping cream

1 t. lemon juice
1/2 c. shredded Swiss cheese
1/2 c. shredded provolone cheese
1/2 c. grated Parmesan cheese
16-oz. pkg. fresh spinach

Fry bacon in a skillet until crisp. Add onion and mushrooms to skillet;
sauté until onion is tender. Add whipping cream, lemon juice and
cheeses. Place spinach in a bowl; top with sautéed ingredients and blend
well. Transfer mixture to a well-greased 2-quart casserole dish. Bake at
350 degrees for 45 minutes to one hour.

Keep a cherished cookbook clean and free of spatters.
Slip it into a gallon-size plastic zipping bag before
cooking up a favorite recipe.

Hot Bacon Brussels Sprouts

Serves 10 to 12

3 lbs. Brussels sprouts, quartered
2 T. olive oil
1 t. salt
10 slices bacon, chopped

1/2 c. balsamic vinegar
2 T. brown sugar, packed
1 t. Dijon mustard

In a large bowl, toss Brussels sprouts with olive oil and salt. Place on a rimmed baking sheet lined with aluminum foil. Bake at 400 degrees for 20 minutes, or until tender. In a large skillet over medium-high heat, cook bacon until crisp. Using a slotted spoon, remove bacon; drain on paper towels. Reserve 1/4 cup drippings in skillet. Add remaining ingredients to skillet. Cook over medium-high heat, stirring frequently, for 6 minutes, or until mixture is reduced by half. Drizzle over sprouts, tossing gently to coat. Sprinkle with bacon.

Potluck dinners are a wonderful way to share fellowship
with family & friends. Why not make a standing date once
a month to try new recipes as well as tried & true favorites?

Scalloped Potatoes

Serves 6

3 potatoes, peeled and sliced
6 slices bacon, halved
1 onion, chopped
3 T. fried chicken coating mix

1/2 t. salt
2 c. milk
1 c. shredded Cheddar cheese

In a saucepan over medium heat, cover potatoes with water and cook until almost tender; drain. Meanwhile, cook bacon and onion in a skillet over medium heat. Drain, reserving 2 tablespoons drippings. Add coating mix, salt and milk to reserved drippings; cook until thickened. Fold potatoes into bacon mixture. Transfer to a greased 3-1/2 quart casserole dish. Bake, covered, at 350 degrees for 30 minutes. Remove cover; top with cheese and bake for another 15 minutes, or until cheese is melted.

Pick up a vintage divided serving dish or two...
they're just right for serving up a choice of
veggie sides without crowding the table.

Country Cabin Potatoes

Makes 10 to 12 servings

4 14-1/2 oz. cans sliced potatoes, drained
2 10-3/4 oz. cans cream of celery soup
16-oz. container sour cream
10 slices bacon, crisply cooked and crumbled
6 green onions, thinly sliced

Place potatoes in a slow cooker. In a bowl, combine remaining ingredients; pour over potatoes and stir gently. Cover and cook on high setting for 4 to 5 hours.

No peeking when there's a casserole in the oven!
Every time the oven door is opened, the temperature drops
at least 25 degrees...dinner will take longer to bake.

Chicken Bacon-Ranch Bake

Makes 4 servings

12-oz. pkg. frozen cauliflower
1/2 lb. boneless, skinless chicken
   breast, cooked and cubed
1 bunch green onions, chopped
2 T. light ranch salad dressing

1-1/2 c. shredded Colby-Jack
   cheese, divided
salt and pepper to taste
2 slices bacon, crisply cooked
   and crumbled

Cook cauliflower according to package directions; drain very well.
In a bowl, combine cauliflower, chicken, green onions, salad dressing,
1-1/4 cups cheese, salt and pepper. Mix well; spoon into an 8"x8" baking
pan sprayed with non-stick vegetable spray. Sprinkle bacon and
remaining cheese on top. Cover and bake at 350 degrees for 30 minutes,
or until heated through and cheese is melted.

Chicken thighs are extra flavorful, juicy and easy on the budget,
but are usually sold with the bone in. To speed up cooking time,
use a sharp knife to make a deep cut on each side of the bone.

Bacon-Swiss BBQ Chicken

Makes 6 servings

6 boneless, skinless chicken breasts	6 slices bacon, halved and crisply cooked
26-oz. bottle barbecue sauce	6 slices Swiss cheese

Place chicken in a slow cooker; cover with barbecue sauce. Cover and cook on low setting for 8 to 9 hours. Arrange 2 halved slices bacon over each piece of chicken; top with cheese slices. Cover and cook on high setting until cheese melts, about 15 minutes.

My theory on housework is, if the item doesn't multiply,
smell, catch on fire, or block the refrigerator door,
let it be. No one cares. Why should you?

– Erma Bombeck

Jalapeño-Bacon Cheese Steak

Makes 8 servings

2 lbs. ground beef chuck
1-3/4 c. soft bread crumbs
3/4 c. beef broth
2 eggs, beaten
1 T. salt
1-1/2 t. pepper

8-oz. pkg. shredded Cheddar
  cheese
8 slices bacon, diced and crisply
  cooked
4 green onions, sliced
2 jalapeño peppers, diced

Place ground beef in a large bowl. In a separate bowl, mix bread crumbs and broth until thoroughly combined. Add bread mixture, eggs, salt and pepper to beef; combine gently. Form into 8 patties. Grill over medium heat for about 8 minutes on each side, or place on a baking sheet and bake at 300 degrees for 30 minutes. Top with cheese, bacon, onions and peppers during the last few minutes of cooking.

A pizza cutter is ideal for dividing up slices of quiche
while it's still in the pie plate.

Ham, Mushroom & Bacon Quiche

Serves 4

6 eggs, beaten
3/4 c. milk
salt and pepper to taste
1 c. shredded Cheddar cheese
2 to 3 slices bacon, crisply
  cooked and crumbled

4 slices deli ham, chopped
4-oz. can sliced mushrooms,
  drained
9-inch pie crust

Whisk together eggs and milk in a medium bowl. Add salt and pepper;
set aside. Sprinkle cheese, bacon, ham and mushrooms on top of crust;
pour egg mixture over top. Bake at 350 degrees for 25 to 30 minutes,
or until a toothpick comes out clean and top is golden.

When a slow-cooker roast recipe gives a range of cooking times like 8 to 10 hours, roasts will be tender after 8 hours and can be sliced neatly. After 10 hours, they will shred...perfect for sandwiches with sauce.

Bacon & Sage Roast Turkey

Makes 8 servings

8 new redskin potatoes, halved
1-1/2 c. baby carrots
1/2 t. garlic-pepper seasoning
6-lb. turkey breast
12-oz. jar roast turkey gravy

2 T. all-purpose flour
4 to 6 slices bacon, crisply
  cooked and crumbled
1 T. Worcestershire sauce
3/4 t. dried sage

Arrange potatoes and carrots in a 6-quart slow cooker; sprinkle with seasoning. Place turkey breast-side up on top of vegetables. In a small bowl, combine gravy, flour, bacon, Worcestershire sauce and sage. Mix well and pour over turkey and vegetables. Cover and cook on low setting for 7 to 9 hours, until juices run clear when pierced.

Get a head start on dinner by peeling and cutting up potatoes the night before. They won't turn dark if you cover them with water before refrigerating them.

Farmhouse Potato Pie

Makes 6 to 8 servings

1 lb. bacon, chopped
1 onion, chopped
8 eggs, beaten
1 lb. potatoes, peeled and grated

2-3/4 c. shredded sharp Cheddar
  cheese
1/2 t. pepper

Cook bacon and onion in a skillet over medium heat until bacon is crisp and onion is transparent, about 8 minutes. Drain mixture well on paper towels. Combine eggs, potatoes, cheese and pepper in a large bowl; stir in bacon mixture. Spread evenly in a greased 13"x9" baking pan. Bake at 350 degrees for 45 minutes, until set in center; cut into squares to serve.

Pour bacon drippings into a jar and store in the fridge.
Add a spoonful or two when cooking hashbrown potatoes,
green beans or pan gravy for a wonderful down-home flavor.

Egg & Bacon Quesadillas

Serves 4

2 T. butter, divided
4 8-inch flour tortillas
5 eggs, beaten
1/2 c. milk
2 8-oz. pkgs. shredded
   Cheddar cheese

6 to 8 slices bacon, crisply
   cooked and crumbled
Optional: salsa, sour cream

Lightly spread about 1/4 teaspoon butter on one side of each tortilla; set aside. In a bowl, beat eggs and milk until combined. Pour egg mixture into a hot, lightly greased skillet; cook and stir over medium heat until done. Remove scrambled eggs to a dish and keep warm. Melt remaining butter in the skillet and add a tortilla, buttered-side down. Layer with 1/4 of the cheese, 1/2 of the eggs and 1/2 of the bacon. Top with 1/4 of the cheese and a tortilla, buttered-side up. Cook one to 2 minutes on each side, until golden. Repeat with remaining ingredients. Cut each into 4 wedges and serve with salsa and sour cream, if desired.

Don't store tomatoes in the refrigerator...they'll quickly
lose their just-picked taste. Instead, keep them on
a pantry shelf or countertop, placed stem-end down.

Peg's Tomato-Bacon Pie

Serves 6 to 8

2 to 3 tomatoes, peeled and sliced
9-inch pie crust, baked
salt and pepper to taste
1/2 c. green onions, chopped
1/3 c. fresh basil, chopped

1/2 c. bacon, crisply cooked
  and crumbled
1 c. mayonnaise
1 c. shredded Cheddar cheese

Layer tomato slices in pie crust. Season to taste with salt and pepper.
Top with onions, basil and bacon. In a bowl, mix together mayonnaise
and cheese; spread over bacon. Bake, uncovered, at 350 degrees for
30 minutes, or until lightly golden. Cut into wedges.

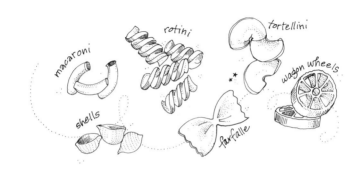

macaroni

rotini

tortellini

wagon wheels

shells

farfalle

Lots of different pasta shapes like bowties, seashells and corkscrew–shaped cavatappi work well in casseroles... why not give a favorite casserole a whole new look?

Bacon Florentine Fettuccine

Makes 4 servings

16-oz. pkg. fettuccine pasta,
uncooked
2 10-oz. pkgs. frozen creamed
spinach
1/2 lb. bacon, crisply cooked
and crumbled

1/8 t. garlic powder
1/2 c. plus 2 T. grated Parmesan
cheese, divided
pepper to taste

Prepare fettuccine in a stockpot as package directs; drain, reserving
3/4 cup of cooking liquid. Microwave spinach as directed on package.
Add spinach, bacon and garlic powder to stockpot. Slowly drizzle
reserved liquid into stockpot until sauce reaches desired consistency.
Return pasta to stockpot and heat through. Transfer to a serving
dish and stir in 1/2 cup cheese. Season with pepper; sprinkle with
remaining cheese.

Fill the sink with hot soapy water when you start dinner
and just toss in pans and utensils as they're used.
Clean-up will be a breeze!

Hashbrown-Bacon Pie

Serves 6

5 eggs
1/2 c. milk
3 c. frozen shredded hashbrowns, thawed
1/3 c. green onion, thinly sliced

1/2 t. salt
1-1/2 c. shredded sharp Cheddar cheese, divided
4 slices bacon, crisply cooked, crumbled and divided

Blend together eggs and milk; stir in hashbrowns, onion and salt. Add one cup cheese and half of the bacon. Pour into a greased 9" pie plate. Bake at 350 degrees for 25 to 30 minutes, until center is set. Sprinkle with remaining bacon and cheese; bake an additional 5 minutes. Cut into wedges.

No self-rising cornmeal in the pantry? For each cup you need,
just mix 3/4 cup plus 3 tablespoons regular cornmeal,
one tablespoon baking powder and 1/2 teaspoon salt.

Tracy's Bacon Cornbread

Makes 8 to 10 servings

1 egg, beaten
1 c. milk
1/2 c. bran cereal, shredded
   or crushed
1 c. yellow cornmeal
1 c. all-purpose flour

2 T. sugar
1-1/2 t. baking powder
Optional: 1/2 t. salt
2 to 3 slices bacon, diced
Garnish: butter

In a large bowl, mix together all ingredients except bacon and butter. Pour into a greased 8"x8" baking pan. Sprinkle bacon over top. Bake at 375 degrees for 30 minutes, or until golden. Cut into squares; serve warm with butter.

Primitive-style wooden cutting boards in fun shapes like pigs, fish or roosters can often be found at tag sales. Put them to use as whimsical party snack servers.

Pull-Apart Bacon Bread

1 t. oil
3/4 c. green pepper, chopped
3/4 c. onion, chopped
3 7-1/2 oz. tubes refrigerated
   buttermilk biscuits

1 lb. bacon, crisply cooked
   and crumbled
1/4 c. butter, melted
1 c. shredded Cheddar cheese

Heat oil in a large skillet; sauté green pepper and onion until tender.
Remove from heat; set aside. Slice biscuits into quarters; place in
a bowl. Add pepper mixture, bacon, butter and cheese; toss until mixed.
Transfer mixture to a greased 10" tube pan; bake at 350 degrees for
30 minutes. Invert onto a serving platter to serve.

Serve fuss-free favorites like Bacon & Cheese Muffins
any time! Everyone can help themselves while
the day's fun is beginning.

Bacon & Cheese Muffins

Serves 6

1/2 lb. bacon, diced
2 c. all-purpose flour
2 t. baking powder
1/4 t. salt
1/4 t. pepper

1-1/4 c. milk
1 egg, beaten
1/4 c. butter, melted and slightly
    cooled
3/4 c. shredded Cheddar cheese

In a skillet over medium heat, cook bacon until crisp; drain on paper towels. Meanwhile, in a large bowl, stir together flour, baking powder, salt and pepper. In a separate bowl, mix together milk, egg and melted butter. Add milk mixture to flour mixture; stir just until moistened. Fold in bacon and cheese just until combined. Fill greased or paper-lined muffin cups 2/3 full. Bake at 400 degrees for 20 to 25 minutes, until lightly golden.

Ovens may vary, so set a kitchen timer when the pan goes into the oven. Check for doneness after the shortest baking time given...if a little more time is needed, be sure to watch carefully.

Bacon Bread Sticks

Makes 2 dozen

1 c. grated Parmesan cheese
2 t. garlic salt
12 slices bacon, halved

24 4-1/2 inch sesame bread
   sticks

Combine Parmesan cheese and garlic salt in a medium bowl; set aside. Wrap each bread stick with a halved slice of bacon, starting at one end and spiraling to other end. Arrange bread sticks on a parchment paper-lined baking sheet. Bake at 350 degrees for 15 minutes, or until bacon is crisp. Remove from oven; immediately roll bread sticks in cheese mixture. Let cool before serving.

Most fruit pies and cobblers can be frozen up to 4 months...
a terrific way to capture the flavor of summer-ripe fruit.
Cool after baking, then wrap in plastic wrap and aluminum
foil before freezing. To serve, thaw overnight in the
fridge and warm in the oven.

Bacon-Apple Pie

Makes 6 servings

3/4 c. brown sugar, packed
2 T. cornstarch
1 T. cinnamon
1/2 t. nutmeg
6 c. Granny Smith apples, peeled,
   cored and thinly sliced

9-inch pie crust, unbaked
10-12 slices thick-cut bacon,
   uncooked

In a large bowl, mix together sugar, cornstarch, cinnamon and nutmeg until well blended. Add apples and toss to coat. Pour apple mixture into pie crust. Criss-cross bacon strips over apple mixture in a lattice pattern. Trim the edges and crimp into the crust to seal. Cover with aluminum foil and bake at 350 degrees for one hour. Remove foil and continue baking for 15 minutes, until bacon is crisp.

Create a charming cake stand with thrift-store finds.
Attach a glass plate with epoxy glue to a short glass
vase or candle stand for a base. Let dry completely
before using...so clever!

Chocolate-Bacon Cupcakes

Makes 2 dozen

2 c. all-purpose flour
3/4 c. plus 1 T. baking cocoa,
   divided
2 c. sugar
1 t. baking powder
2 t. baking soda
1/2 t. salt

2 eggs, beaten
1 c. strong brewed coffee, cooled
1 c. buttermilk
1/2 c. oil
12 slices bacon, crisply cooked,
   crumbled and divided
Garnish: chocolate frosting

In a large bowl, stir together flour, 3/4 cup baking cocoa, sugar, baking powder, baking soda and salt. Make a well in the center; add eggs, coffee, buttermilk and oil. Stir just until blended; mix in 3/4 of bacon. Spoon batter into greased or paper-lined muffin cups, filling 2/3 full. Bake at 375 degrees for 20 to 25 minutes, until tops spring back when lightly pressed. Set muffin tin on a wire rack to cool. Frost cupcakes; sprinkle with remaining bacon and dust with remaining cocoa.

INDEX

INDEX

Our Story

Back in 1984, we were next-door neighbors raising our families in the little town of Delaware, Ohio. Two moms with small children, we were looking for a way to do what we loved and stay home with the kids too. We had always shared a love of home cooking and making memories with family & friends and so, after many a conversation over the backyard fence, **Gooseberry Patch** was born.

We put together our first catalog at our kitchen tables, enlisting the help of our loved ones wherever we could. From that very first mailing, we found an immediate connection with many of our customers and it wasn't long before we began receiving letters, photos and recipes from these new friends. In 1992, we put together our very first cookbook, compiled from hundreds of these recipes and, the rest, as they say, is history.

Hard to believe it's been almost 40 years since those kitchen-table days! From that original little **Gooseberry Patch** family, we've grown to include an amazing group of creative folks who love cooking, decorating and creating as much as we do. Today, we're best known for our homestyle, family-friendly cookbooks, now recognized as national bestsellers.

One thing's for sure, we couldn't have done it without our friends all across the country. Each year, we're honored to turn thousands of your recipes into our collectible cookbooks. Our hope is that each book captures the stories and heart of all of you who have shared with us. Whether you've been with us since the beginning or are just discovering us, welcome to the **Gooseberry Patch** family!

Jo Ann & Vickie

Visit our website anytime
www.gooseberrypatch.com

Email

1·800·854·6673